DICK

STRAWBRIDGE

A Detailed Biography

John Brooklyn

Table of Contents

In the Beginning

Jennifer and George Strawbridge welcomed their third child, Richard Francis Strawbridge, into the world on September 3, 1959. He is affectionately known as *Dick* and holds the distinction of being the third child in a loving family of seven siblings.

He was born in Burma but spent most of his childhood in County Antrim, Northern Ireland. Because his father worked in the oil sector in the Middle East and the Far East, his mother was responsible for raising all of their children alone. Dick's mother used wooden spoons as a kind of punishment for him and his siblings, and they are buried in the garden where he spent his childhood. When she wasn't looking, they'd sneak off with the spoons and hide them. He was also taught the age-old virtues of gallantry and female deference. Despite his engineering background, Dick says he still has plenty to learn about women. He began his formal education at Bangor Grammar Prep School and then continued it from 1971 to 1976 at Ballyclare High School.

To prepare for a career in the military, he enrolled in and rose through the ranks of leadership at Welbeck DSFC, a Nottinghamshire sixth-form college.

Career Journey

A member of the British Army since 1979, Dick Strawbridge graduated from the Royal Military Academy Sandhurst in 1977.

He enrolled in the Royal Corps of Signals in 1980 after finishing a study in signals and communication.

After that, he attended Shrivenham Military College for three years to get a degree in electronics and electrical engineering from the Royal Military College of Science.

He started as a second lieutenant in April 1981, then a captain in October 1985, and finally a major in September 1991. For his exemplary work in Northern Ireland, he was awarded an MBE from the British government in 1993. As of June 1999, he is a lieutenant colonel. He served for nearly twenty years until retiring as a lieutenant colonel in the army in 2001.

At the behest of his family, he tried out for *the Scrapheap Challenge* on Channel 4 when he was still serving as a colonel in the army. Competitors in the program were tasked with using only items found in the scrapyard to create a functional machine capable of performing a certain purpose. As the *Yellow Team Leader* for the first six episodes of *Scrapheap Challenge*, he got his start in the television industry. The team's selection of him as a leader and a competitor was heavily influenced by his leadership qualities, his charisma, and his technical expertise. In 2000, he and his brothers David and Bobby, as members of Team Brothers in Arms, won the third season. In the eleventh season (2009/2010), he took over as the show's primary host from Robert Llewellyn. He was also a regular on the American version of Junkyard *Mega-Wars*, where he led his side to victory in 2003.

Crafty Tricks of War, a six-part BBC Two program he hosted in 2004, had him recreating and testing some of the most bizarre military innovations.

In 2005, he joined Ferne Cotton on another BBC Two program called *Geronimo*. The candidates were given the task of building the most outlandish devices ever shown on television. He also played a significant part in the BBC's coverage of the 60th anniversary of *D-Day*.

The Green Path

Three seasons of *It's Not Easy Being Green* aired on BBC Two from 2006 and 2009 and featured Dick Strawbridge, his then-wife Brigit, and their children James and Charlotte. The show emphasized sustainable, eco-friendly lifestyle choices.

The first season followed the Strawbridge family as they relocated from Malvern, Worcestershire, to Tywardreath, Cornwall, and into *Newhouse Farm*, a 400-year-old listed structure. With the assistance of their newfound beer-drinking student friends and the local merchants, the family plants crops, re-tiles the roof and builds a wooden aqueduct from a stream to a water wheel in the hopes that the water wheel would provide enough energy to power the house's lights.

Season each season, the family worked to make their home and garden more sustainable and eco-friendly. Two pigs with foreboding names like *Christmas* and *New Year* are added to the family, and a greenhouse is built, complete with a custom heatsink designed by Dick and constructed from recycled bottle glass to keep the greenhouse warm. Dick hooks up a generator to the water wheel that powers the home's lighting, and the family reaps a bountiful crop for the first time. The fourth episode of the first season features the installation of a heating distribution system to disperse the heat from the efficient wood-burning stoves throughout the home and remove any remaining moisture. Biodiesel is made by Dick and Jim from chip fat. The heating distribution system is failing as winter approaches; the wood burners can't keep up with the brisk winds in Cornwall. As Dick's children attend college attend college, they continue to spread the green message beyond. The water mains are cut off and replaced with a wind turbine-powered pump for the well at the garden's base.

The water wheel and heat sink are both effective in reducing temperatures. To supplement the wood burners in the early spring and late fall, Dick sets up a solar hot water system. On the 28th of December, Mike the farmer, and Chris the butcher assist the butcher and kill the pigs on the farm. A spit-roasted pig is the main attraction of the annual *New Year's Eve* feast. A composting toilet and a second wind turbine are built in the season one finale. Making her moisturizer is how Brigit breaks into the beauty industry. Patrick Whitefield, a permaculture specialist, and Donnachadh McCarthy, a green auditor, give the family their input during the ecological evaluation. Jim Milner and Anda Phillips, two pals, helped them out, as did, at various times, an army of friends and family. The series was accompanied by a book by Dick Strawbridge titled *It's Not Easy Being Green.*

Season 2 focused more on the Strawbridges' efforts to help others become green than on their own home. In the pilot episode, Dick installs a ground-source heat pump and a wind turbine for a household. Later, with the aid of his son James, Dick assists another family in growing and cultivating fresh produce for a youngster with numerous food sensitivities. In the second episode, Dick visits Bath to see a neglected urban garden transformed into a sustainable space with the use of solely free recycled materials. Later, Dick assists a family in Cornwall in constructing an eco-friendly campground. The third episode features a return to two prior projects: a green urban garden in Bath and an eco-campground in Cornwall. Later, Dick pays a visit to a couple who left urban life for a simpler life in rural Scotland.

Next, Dick goes to the house of a woman who built it in the '30s and wants to paint it in an eco-friendly manner while preserving its unique character. Later, he assists a father and daughter in Northampton with the installation of a solar panel. He also thinks of a brilliant way to help a guy who wants a solar panel but can't afford one. The group later encounters a lady who has adopted a green lifestyle by, among other things, heating her home with wood and adopting non-toxic methods of personal care.

To check on Jake and Candy's wind turbine, Dick travels back to their Cornwall eco-campsite. The difficulty of adjusting to living in a conservation area later becomes apparent to Zannah and Arthur. Later, Dick goes to a beautiful home in southern England, but he discovers the heating expenses are over the roof. Later, they go back to check in with a lady who has been green-renovating her 1930s home. In the last episode, Dick advises a primary school on how to reduce its water expenditures. Later, Dick and Jim assist a mechanic in powering his four-wheel drive with a biodiesel engine that runs on used vegetable oil.

The third season, which aired in 2009, they followed a more *magazine* format, with recurring features such as an in-depth look at the *green* renovation of a townhouse throughout the show and interviews with celebrities about the eco-friendliness (or lack thereof) of their practices.

The first episode features the installation of solar PV panels on the outbuildings at *Newhouse Farm*, a demonstration of natural deodorant on a group of half-naked footballers, a look at eco-swimming pools by series regular Lauren Laverne, and an interview with Phil Tufnell about how eco-friendly his lifestyle is conducted by Dick, who has taken on a more prominent role as co-presenter. After that, Dick investigates the situation of the honey bee, James builds an earth oven with his buddy Duncan Glendinning from the *Thoughtful Bread Company*, James and Brigit tend the garden at a London excavation, and Dick chats with Alex James, a member of the band Blur.

In the third episode, Dick and James kill a few pigs for home consumption before taking them to the abattoir. Dick chats with Lauren Laverne, as Jon Kay examines the plastics recycling market. At the same time, London's excavation moves on with the installation of a huge rainwater collecting system. After that, James and Dick construct a geodesic dome at *Newhouse Farm*, Lauren explores the cutting edge of eco-fashion, Dick chats with CBBC hosts Sam and Mark, and Jon Kay investigates the *logic* underlying zoning laws.

In the sixth episode, Dick and James go to the Newhouse Farm to gather apples for cider. Lauren goes foraging with specialist Carol Hunt, and Jilly Goolden is brought in for an eco-test. Dick and James had an environmentally friendly suggestion concerning soap nuts, and the London evocative project got some more chicks. In the season finale, James talks to Hunter Davies about cheap living, Phill Jupitus is this week's eco-test guest, and Dick and James pay their final visit to the London excavation while preparing one of their home-raised turkeys and organic vegetables for a special lunch to be delivered on Bodmin Moor.

Many scenes from all three seasons of *It's Not Easy Being Green* was shot at *Newhouse Farm*, the home of Dick and James Strawbridge. The Strawbridges taught eco-friendly topics including biodiesel production, wind power generation, water power generation, and eco-engineering on their farm as part of their eco-courses.

The Chateau Journey

The television series offers a captivating glimpse into the extraordinary journey of Dick Strawbridge and Angel Adoree as they navigate the intricate balance of raising their two young children while embarking on an ambitious venture. Their journey is nothing short of remarkable as they simultaneously establish a wedding and event planning company, all while undertaking the colossal task of renovating the enchanting 19th-century *Château de la Motte-Husson*.

Situated in the picturesque French countryside, the *Château de la Motte-Husson* stands as a testament to architectural elegance, boasting a design steeped in the Neo-Renaissance style. In a bygone era, this fortified castle served as the residence of the esteemed

Baglion de la Dufferie family, its illustrious history is woven into the very fabric of its stone walls. A defining moment in the *château's* architectural evolution came in the 19th century when Countess Louise-Dorothée de Baglion de la Dufferie commissioned the creation of the exquisite facade that graces the castle to this day.

However, the passage of time saw the *château* endure periods of vacancy and neglect, its grandeur fading into the background until the fateful year of 2015. It was then that Dick Strawbridge and his wife Angela, fueled by an unshakable passion for historic preservation and a shared vision of creating a place of wonder and enchantment, took ownership of this grand estate.

The *Château de la Motte-Husson* has risen to fame not only for its historical significance but also for its enchanting idiosyncrasies that beguile the imagination. Among these features, the *taxidermied wolf* facsimile stands as a unique emblem of the château's mystique, intriguing and captivating visitors with its intriguing presence. The walled garden, meanwhile, weaves a tapestry of colors and fragrances, a testament to the timeless allure of nature that graces this exceptional estate.

Intricately entwined with both personal and architectural history, the *Château de la Motte-Husson* has become a canvas for Dick Strawbridge and Angel Adoree to paint their dreams, embodying their journey of family, entrepreneurship, and a passionate commitment to the preservation of this extraordinary piece of history. It stands as a living testament to the power of dedication and vision, offering a window into the captivating world of *Château de la Motte-Husson* and the indomitable spirit of its devoted stewards.

Angel Adoree, who has a hospitality business called *The Vintage Patisserie* and appeared on *Dragon's Den* in 2010 to seek investment for it, adds a creative element and flair to the show by bringing her sense of style and interior-decorating expertise to the *château* and sharing the hosts' interest in hosting and entertaining to create memorable experiences for their guests. Adoree, whose birth name is Angela Newman, spent her childhood on Canvey Island, where her family owns and operates a jewelry store.

The Strawbridge family finally located the abandoned 19th-century property with moat and pepper-pot towers that would become their lifelong home after years of seeking. They were resolved to revive it despite the warnings in the 200 pages of acquisition paperwork. In the first season, Dick and Angel go on a mission to turn the abandoned *château* into a viable house again by bringing modern conveniences like plumbing, heating, and electricity to the property's 45 previously unoccupied rooms. Dick and Angel had just nine months to arrange their wedding and renovate the *Chateau* before the big day. Downstairs, a new kitchen was erected, and walls were torn down to create museums. As the wedding date approached, they devoted their attention to transforming three levels of the castle into elegant accommodations for their guests.

The pair built a do-it-yourself pig-roaster in the second season's last episode as they prepared for their first paid event at the castle. Their three-year-old son, Arthur, had his school debut in an episode. On the other side, Angel designed a Versailles-themed basement bathroom. Together, they came up with a scheme to increase their income by fishing in the moat and setting up a lift in the turret. Angel prepares for Christmas by cleaning the house and cooking a feast for her English relatives who are flying in for the holiday.

Twenty rooms need mending, and Angel and Dick are on the case in the third season. Dick is building a wall around their yard, while Angel is decorating a boudoir. The suggestions made by guests during a meal are highlighted. Dick has been working to clean up and prepare the barn for the upcoming wedding season.

In the fourth season, the summer is jam-packed with work on the gardens and stables, as well as the planning and execution of seven weddings and fourteen food-lovers weekends. Over the moat, Angel proposes to construct a floating geodesic dome. As a family, they honor Dick on his special day. The stucco of the chateau is in bad shape, so Dick is working on it while Angel completes the geodesic dome over the moat. The family put it to good use by having a campout in the backyard.

In the fifth season, Angel and Dick, the proprietors of a French castle, reopen their doors to begin developing a luxury glamping experience. They have to arrange several tasks despite obstacles like constant rain. Angel plans a vacation to Paris with her daughter Dorothy, decorates the tower of the castle, and prepares a beautiful attic studio. When Dick tries to build a parkour fitness track, he runs into several snags. Events season, heat, melted wedding cakes, school breaks, a broken boat, and a lake popular for boating all come into play during the summer. They have been plowing a wildflower field and fixing up an old coach house in preparation for opening Cafe Grandma as winter approaches. They also turn a pigpen into a goose house. Once everything is ready, they have a lovely Christmas at the chateau with their loved ones, complete with Dick's walnut wine and a huge Christmas tree.

Angel transforms the utility room and certain dumping places in the basement of the chateau into an events kitchen during the sixth season's *down* season. When they attempt to put in a big oven, they run into a lot of problems. Angel also finds some old wallpaper hiding beneath the stairs and purchases a little canal boat in need of repair. They should also complete the construction of a wildflower meadow.

A circus tent shows up at the chateau even though it's peak wedding season. Angel and Dick also built two enormous aviaries and a pond full of water lilies. Angel and the crew are also preparing for a lavish celebration of Angel's parents' 50th wedding anniversary during the sweltering *French summer*.

Meanwhile, Dick visits Wales in search of a replacement car.

After the summer, the *chateau* will host a Citron van festival. The couple from the *château* is now sprucing up their *Mademoiselle Daisy*-themed *former wedding bus*.

Angel and Dick decided to renovate the *chateau's* old tack room into a magnificent entryway by knocking down walls and installing a new floor. They also started renovating a riverboat that they had just purchased to use as more guest rooms. It's that time of year again, and the chateau is bustling with preparations for Christmas celebrations with family, friends, and visitors.

In the seventh season, Dick and Angel finally get to work on their never-ending to-do list, beginning with one of the ancient barns, after a long, hot, and stressful summer with no visitors, weddings, or celebrations at the chateau. Dick intends to use the remaining of the berries to produce sloe gin. Angel immediately sets about restoring the ceiling and constructing a library in the pepper pot tower.

Dick and Angel have begun remodeling the lavatory in the moat's ancient washhouse. When they come to a massive ditch, Angel's imagination goes wild. They also restore their classic motorcycles. With no visitors to host, Dick and Angel put their roofing expert and some pre-owned Welsh slate to work on the orangery and make a surprising discovery.

To honor Dick and Angel on their fifth wedding anniversary, the entire family pitched in to construct an open kitchen, set up a pop-up restaurant in the orangery, and arrange for a magical carriage delivery. The Strawbridge family uses a 19th-century ledger they discover in the attic as inspiration for their winter paradise, replete with an ice rink, in this holiday special.

As they continue to restore their 19th-century house, Angel, Arthur, and Dorothy tell more entrancing stories from the *Chateau* in the eighth season. The epidemic has forced them to postpone their celebrations, including weddings, for a second year running. As their most ambitious job yet, they opted to work on the home's exterior, namely the roof and outside walls. Construction rapidly began in and around the château. With the original roof in need of repair, re-tiling, and insulation, Dick and Angel begin their largest, messiest, and most costly project to date at the *chateau*. In the walled garden, they forage for ingredients to prepare mint tea and rainbow sweetcorn relish, transforming the preserves closet in the process.

Garden diversions, such as homemade gigantic dominoes and a treasure hunt throughout the *Chateau* grounds, are included during Dick and Angel's garden party for Arthur and Dorothy's guests. Jelly with ice cream and Angela's signature rose petal and honey sandwiches are two of her delicious creations. Meanwhile, the scaffolding has arrived, and for the first time in 150 years, work will be done to re-slate the roof of the *Chateau*.

Angel comes up with the brilliant idea of building a *mezzanine* when she realizes that Arthur and Dorothy, being teenagers, would soon want their beds. While Dick and Angel continue to re-slate the roof, they also tear down walls and rebuild them, save the old wallpaper, make furniture out of the kid's old clothing, and find time to harvest strawberries from the garden.

Angel learns that the *chateau* has a massive attic that spans the length of the structure and rises to the peak of the roof. While Dick appreciates the extra closet space, Angel sees the potential for a cool space-themed pub with stargazing terraces. The project's novel use of insulation, a new staircase, and skylights paid off when a clear night offered an opportunity to gaze at the heavens in search of meteors.

Angel decides to bring the walls of the *Chateau* back to their former grandeur, so he uses computer mock-ups to attempt to choose a hue that would work. They discover a part of a historic cider-making contraption while cleaning the pigsty and set out to locate the remainder of it. The newfound knowledge motivates the family to start collecting apples to press their juice.

The stone balustrade that lines the front steps, the metal awnings over the windows, and the wooden double entrance door with its intricate metal tracery are all in need of restoration. The former jeweler father of Angel steps in to attempt to duplicate the massive door key that dates back 150 years. To get some razor clams, the family takes a trip to the beach.

The *Strawbridges* later go to France's Alsace region, where they sample regional specialties. Back at the chateau, they use their newfound Christmas spirit to throw a spectacular holiday party.

In the finale, the *château* reopens after being shuttered for two years. Dick and Angel are scrambling to catch up in time for wedding season, and the *Atelier de Mariage* is taking form as a result. Angel and Dorothy make confetti cones out of dried petals, while Dick and Arthur prepare a seven-course wedding brunch, and the *chateau* has its first wedding in almost two years. The family's focus shifts to the cherished walled garden each spring. They want to restore a folly from the nineteenth century that has been covered in ivy and is located on the wall facing north. Dick has to clear out the overgrown bamboo grove so Angel can work his magic inside.

Due to the summer's drought and high temperatures, the water level in the moat has dropped to an all-time low, and the family has had to pull together to preserve the fish. The recent makeover of the folly in the walled garden has made Dick and Angel realize the possibilities of the space surrounding it. They want to renovate the area by building a new patio for gatherings with friends and family. The peach tree in the walled garden finally bears fruit after eight years, and Dick, Angel, Arthur, and Dorothy can't wait to enjoy the first peach the Strawbridge family has ever produced. Dick and Angel started preparing for a monumental 50th birthday celebration for their best friend and mutual introduction, Sophie.

Dick and Angel go to the attic's last undiscovered room. They find an ancient train set hidden in the dust and cobwebs of the castle, among other unexpected gems. Dick and Angel knew their kids would outgrow their playroom quickly, so they intended to furnish it with both old and new games. Dick and Angel have a new project on their hands in the form of a vintage *Renault* 4CV from the 1950s that needs some TLC.

Dick and Angel build a glass greenhouse at their home to enjoy the winter weather. In the meanwhile, the chateau is preparing for its largest wedding to date, so there is a great deal of preparation to be done. It's time to sort out the invitations for the big Christmas party that Dick and Angel are throwing for all of their family and friends, and they feature fudge, sparkles, and a tin can. *The Strawbridges* wrap off their trip with a reflective look back, setting the scene against a festive *outdoor* Christmas dinner with plenty of relatives.

In their pursuit of finding the perfect place to call home, Dick Strawbridge made the strategic decision to involve Channel 4 in documenting their house-hunting adventures. This choice was not made lightly, as the couple, responsible for the upbringing of their two young children, Arthur and Dorothy, had been on a quest for a suitable abode for an extensive four-year period. Unlike many other home improvement programs where such arrangements are premeditated, the partnership with Channel 4 offered them the opportunity to share their journey without the upfront planning that often accompanies such endeavors.

The financial aspects of this ambitious undertaking were undoubtedly substantial, and Channel 4's involvement in funding the documentary provided a welcome relief from this considerable burden. However, it's essential to note that the decision to collaborate with the network was not solely motivated by monetary considerations. The exposure garnered from the show's promotion, combined with the remuneration for Dick Strawbridge's role as presenter, allowed them to maintain their cherished status as a sought-after venue for weddings and other special events. It's a testament to the power of television as a medium to transform fortunes and offer a platform for pursuing one's passions.

The forthcoming ninth season of this captivating journey is poised to debut on Channel 4 in the United Kingdom in October 2022. This season is particularly special, as it marks the culmination of an impressive nine-season run. It's with the gracious consent of Dick and Angel Strawbridge that the decision was made to draw the curtain on this remarkable series, signaling that this ninth season will be the grand finale, leaving an indelible mark on the hearts of the viewers who have accompanied them on this extraordinary odyssey.

A large number of British homebuyers have been drawn to the exhibition because of the relatively low prices and little demand for similar houses in France. At the beginning of their home quest in France, Dick and Angel were only interested in more modest properties like tiny farmhouses.

However, as they saw the cheap costs now available, they quickly changed their focus to purchasing a castle. They paid £280,000 (about £330,305 in 2021) for a 12-acre (4.9-hectare) *chateau* in 2015, which is 10 times bigger than the typical British residence. The property also has 45 rooms, a walled garden, and a moat. Despite the obvious benefits, viewers have been made aware of the substantial human work necessary, as well as the hefty repair and operating expenses, which may become exorbitant for those seeking to build a company out of these castles, thanks to the program.

The pair announced in December 2022 that their new travel series, *Escape to the Chateau: Secret France*, about their search for the remarkable and unexpected in *France's* past, will premiere in the following year. Four one-hour episodes were planned for the project, which was a collaboration between *Two Rivers Media, Channel 4, and the Strawbridges'* firm, *Chateau TV*. The series was canceled, unfortunately.

In a surprising turn of events in 2023, news emerged that the dynamic *Chateau* duo, Dick and Angel Strawbridge, had been relieved of their duties at Channel 4. This unexpected development was prompted by the network's decision to launch an inquiry into their behavior, spurred by growing concerns surrounding the *Strawbridge*. This investigation ultimately culminated in Channel 4 severing their professional ties with the beloved pair.

The precise nature of the concerns that led to this dramatic separation remained shrouded in mystery. While the *Deadline* publication took the initiative to probe further into the situation, reaching out to three former coworkers of the *Strawbridge*, the intricacies of the claims against them remained elusive. What did surface, however, was the revelation that conflicts had arisen between the *Strawbridge* and the program's producers, but the exact details of these clashes remained undisclosed.

This unexpected chapter in the lives of Dick and Angel Strawbridge serves as a reminder that even within the realms of television and entertainment, challenges and controversies can disrupt the course of a seemingly idyllic journey. The intrigue surrounding their departure from Channel 4 has left fans and the industry at large speculating about the circumstances that led to this surprising turn of events, ultimately raising more questions than answers.

Two Rivers' relationship with Dick and Angel's *Chateau TV* has been worsening for some time, according to a person who was briefed on the matter and spoke to *Deadline*. Tensions arose when we had to shoot some extra scenes while the *Strawbridge* was in the middle of a major renovation. Reports of disagreements over production costs have been circulating, with rumors of an overrun on the 2020/21 season of *Escape to the Chateau: Make Do and Mend* spreading suspicion.

A Channel 4 representative indicated that the network has chosen not to include Dick and Angel in any future projects after conducting an internal investigation. *The Strawbridges* did not provide any statement in response to our inquiry. When asked about the charges, the couple's spokesperson denied them. It has been confirmed by Two Rivers that they will no longer be working with Dick and Angel, but no more details were provided.

It's not the first time a producer has butted heads with the *Strawbridge; Two Rivers* is just the latest. After four seasons of *Escape To The Chateau*, the team decided to break ways with the show's creators and producers at *Spark Media Partners*. While the ninth and final season of *Escape To The Chateau* was running in December 2022, the breakup occurred at the same time.

Behind the scenes, however, insiders say the *Strawbridge* would battle with producers despite their pleasant family image. In their own homes, they will not stand for being remotely governed or ordered about. The couple's on-screen demeanor doesn't match their genuine characteristics, since several eyewitnesses have heard them cursing at others. The couple's alleged abuse of the staff was revealed in 2021 by *The Times of London*. In one recording, Angel is heard calling a producer a *f*****g c**t* when the latter complains about Angel's treatment of him. A spokeswoman for *Strawbridge* at the time refuted some of the charges, which were characterized as historical and connected to creative *tensions* with erstwhile producer Spark Media. Not everyone is worried about what they're doing. In his role as producer and director for the last two seasons of *Escape To The Chateau*, Jonathan Hales praised the cast and crew for being *warm and welcoming.*

French viewers will never get to watch the *Chateau* series, despite its international popularity. It's because the famous couple specifically said that they did not want the program shown in their native nation when they signed on to participate in it. They made this decision so that they wouldn't be labeled a *celebrity couple* in France and could keep their privacy.

Of course, word of the show's popularity has spread across the little town of Martigne-sur-Mayenne where the *chateau* is situated, but Dick prefers to keep his fame at a low simmer.

After making a notable debut in the realm of broadcasting with an enthralling one-time appearance on the BBC Two series *Coast* back in 2006, wherein he embarked on a deep exploration of the intricate workings of the *Middlesbrough Transporter Bridge*, Dick Strawbridge rekindled his connection with the program in the subsequent year, 2007. His return to the show wasn't merely a casual one; it was a momentous comeback where he undertook the emotionally charged and intellectually demanding task of unraveling the poignant and unfortunate history of *Exercise Tiger*.

This moment in his broadcasting career was undeniably a turning point, highlighting his multifaceted talents and profound knowledge. It showcased his capacity to tackle not only the marvels of engineering and coastal landscapes, as seen with the *Middlesbrough Transporter Bridge*, but also the solemn *and* significant aspects of history, as witnessed in his exploration of *Exercise Tiger*. This aptly illustrated his versatility as a presenter and his unwavering commitment to educating and enlightening his audience on a broad spectrum of subjects.

Subsequently, Strawbridge became a recurring presence on the show, serving as a guest host in not just one but three consecutive seasons, namely 2010, 2011, and 2012. In these episodes, the program retained its unwavering focus on the picturesque and historically rich shorelines of the United Kingdom, as well as the adjacent countries that share these coastal wonders.

However, one of the standout moments in Strawbridge's involvement with *Coast* occurred in the July 2009 episode, where he assumed the role of an intrepid explorer and educator. In this particular installment, *Strawbridge* embarked on a journey of discovery as he meticulously analyzed the topography and historical significance of the Normandy landing beaches. This in-depth exploration not only added depth to the program but also showcased his commitment to shedding light on pivotal historical moments through the lens of coastal landscapes. It was a testament to his passion for educating and entertaining audiences about the fascinating world of coastal regions and their historical importance.

In addition to his captivating role as the host of *The Big Idea*, where he skillfully evaluated and put home-made inventions to the test, Dick Strawbridge extended his television presence with a prominent role in the enlightening five-part documentary series known as *The Re-Inventors*. This engaging series found its home on the UK digital channel UKTV History and made its highly anticipated premiere during the second week of December 2006.

Each installment of *The Re-Inventors* featured Strawbridge, often alongside his talented son James, embarking on a mission of innovation with a modest budget of £500 at their disposal. Armed with their portable workshop and a passion for history, they meticulously recreated significant inventions from the past. The real magic unfolded when they pitted their recreated innovations against their original counterparts in a rigorous test of functionality and ingenuity. This fascinating and hands-on approach allowed viewers to witness firsthand the evolution of technology and appreciate the remarkable achievements of inventors throughout history.

Furthermore, fans of Dick Strawbridge's work had the pleasure of occasionally catching episodes of *Crafty Tricks of War* on UKTV History. This additional program provided a unique perspective on the ingenious tactics and innovations that have been employed in the realm of warfare, shedding light on the intersection of history and craftiness in times of conflict. Dick Strawbridge's television endeavors are a testament to his passion for exploration, invention, and the unending quest to breathe new life into historical innovations, all while engaging and educating his dedicated audience.

He took over as host of the National Geographic series Planet Mechanics in 2008. Strawbridge appeared on Robert Llewellyn's *CarPool* online series in November of 2009. In each episode, he gives a guest a ride in an environmentally friendly automobile while interviewing with them.

The following year, he competed on Celebrity Masterchef and promptly got himself severely ill by eating a *dodgy oyster* on the program. Along with Christine Hamilton and Lisa Faulkner, he made it to the show's final three. In 2010, Dick and James Strawbridge released two books: *Self-Sufficiency in the Twenty-First Century* and *Practical Self-Sufficiency: The Complete Guide to Sustainable Living*. In the same year,

Strawbridge was featured on the *Bargain Hunt Children in Need Special*.

In his 2011 series *The Hungry Sailors*, he once again brought the concepts of family and food together. The ITV shows featured the father-and-son team of Dick and James Strawbridge as they sailed the British coast in their boat, the Morwenna, in search of new and exciting culinary experiences by visiting local food producers and, at the end of each episode, challenging them to a cooking competition aboard the boat.

The second season of The *Hungry Sailors* was shot on and around the Cornish coast in 2012, including the Channel Islands and the Isles of Scilly. The show debuted in 2013. That same year, they also hosted a cuisine show on ITV called *Saturday Farm*.

The father and son team launched the *Made at Home cookbook* series in 2012 and 2013 to teach others how to make delicious food and drinks at home.

In 2013, Dick Strawbridge also hosted the Channel 5 series *Beat the Ancestors*, in which he tasked a group of contemporary engineers with recreating and improving upon some of history's most remarkable technologies.

The three of them set out on a 25-mile (40-km) trek across the Berkshire Mountains for National Geographic's adventure series *Dirty Rotten Survival* in 2015. *Trainspotting Live*, a three-part BBC Four series that premiered in July 2016, confirmed him as a co-host. Participants in this series were challenged to submit their train sighting film and locate a legendary engine dubbed *The Holy Grail of the Rail*. During one broadcast, the program was criticized for misidentifying a train and airing what seemed to be a prerecorded video as live.

For the 2017 Channel 4 miniseries *Cabins in the Wild*, he teamed together with master craftsman *Will Hardie*. In the program, contestants worked to construct an outdoor *pop-up hotel* comprised of eight separate *cabins* with a variety of themes. There was a competition to construct rustic cottages to open a hotel in the countryside, and eight entrants were chosen. Both of the hosts built their cottages, too.

The Biggest Little Railway in the World, a Channel 4 miniseries documentary from 2018, chronicled an effort to build the longest model railway in history in Scotland and was hosted by the star of *The Chateau.* He was in charge of engineering it as well.

The hit film Escape to the *Chateau* spawned a spinoff series called *Escape to the Chateau DIY,* in which Dick and Angel help British families buy and restore their *French chateaux.* The show's airing years were 2018–2020. Starting in 2021, the show will be called *Château DIY* and will be narrated by Adjoa Andoh.

The 2020 spinoff *Escape to the Chateau: Make Do and Mend* also has him serving as executive producer.

Their transition to living in France was chronicled in a book released in 2018 called *Chateau: The Beginning*. Another book, *A Year at the Castle* in 2020, followed, expanding upon the family's first year at the castle in even more detail.

The Strawbridges took their *Dare to Do It Tour* down in February of 2023. The tour, which kicked off in Edinburgh in 2022, gives visitors a chance to learn interesting details about the love story that led a man and a woman, who met in 2010, to restore a fairytale castle and turn it into a successful, dynamic business. The schedule spanned from February 12th, 2023, to March 9th, 2023, and featured performances and book signings. In February and March of 2022, they toured the United Kingdom for a similar *Dare to Do It* event.

In 2024, the pair also hopes to go on a trip to the United States and Canada.

Personal Life

Both James and Charlotte were born to Dick Strawbridge and his first wife, Brigit A. Weine. The pair officially split up in 2010 and the reason behind their split remains unknown. The Chateau star went on to start another marital journey with Angela Newman in 2015. Angel first came to the limelight after she pitched her website and company, *The Vintage Patisserie*, on the 2010 episode of *"Dragon's Den,"* where Deborah Meaden and Theo Paphitis offered to invest £100,000. She started the Vintage company in 2005 in London, then in 2015, it was moved to the château that she and her husband own in the Pays de la Loire area of France. Together, they have two beautiful kids, Arthur and Dorothy.

Dick has been extremely open with the public about the age difference between him and his beautiful spouse, Angel. He once said in an interview that he has often told his wife that whenever he dies, she should move on without him. He said this recognizing the fact that he has only a few years to live on. Angel felt quite brokenhearted by it and wished he could live for 30 more years. There is a 19-year age difference between the Chateau couple. Dick Strawbridge is currently in his sixth decade of living while Angel is 45 years old. Dick had already started making arrangements for his burial, saying that he wanted to be laid to rest close to his current residence in France.

The couple became well-known when their château was renovated and used as a wedding destination. Unfortunately, they've had issues with trespassers on their property and have had to ask a visitor to leave before. The current market value of the Château is around £2,000,000.

In 2010, Strawbridge received an Honorary Doctor of Science degree from Plymouth University. He also adheres to Presbyterian beliefs.

While Dick has created a career in television, he has also written books. In 2012, Dick and his oldest son James released a book series which are *Made at Home: Eggs & Poultry* and *Made at Home: Preserves*. Together with his wife, Angel, Dick has also released novels. In 2018, they published their first book together, titled *Chateau: The Beginning*, which provided an interesting look at their life in Pays-de-la-Loire, France. Their second book, *A Year at the Chateau*, recounting their first year in their magnificent mansion, came out in April of 2021.

Summary

Engineer, environmentalist, and TV host Dick Strawbridge was also a lieutenant colonel in the British Army. For nearly twenty years, he served in the army, climbing through the ranks from platoon commander to lieutenant colonel. For his efforts in that region, the United Kingdom recognized him with an MBE in 1993. His career in television really started during his time in the military. He made his television debut on the program Scrapheap Challenge, first as a participant and then as a host. In the years that followed, he appeared on programs including "It's Not Easy Being Green," "Coast," "The Hungry Sailors," and "Celebrity Masterchef." His most famous program, however, is called Escape To The castle, and it follows his family as they relocate to a rundown French castle from the nineteenth century. The program chronicles their efforts to restore the château to its former splendor. Dick has also written novels on their time at the chateau with his son and with Angel.

Printed in Great Britain
by Amazon

42988822R00030